Strange Flowers

Bryan Byrdlong

Strange Flowers

YESYES BOOKS *Portland*

ISBN 978-1-946303-02-8

PRINTED IN THE UNITED STATES OF AMERICA

PUBLISHED BY YESYES BOOKS
1631 NE BROADWAY ST #121
PORTLAND, OR 97232

YESYESBOOKS.COM

◤

KMA SULLIVAN, PUBLISHER

KARAH KEMMERLY, MANAGING EDITOR

GALE MARIE THOMPSON, SENIOR EDITOR, BOOK DEVELOPMENT

ALBAN FISCHER, GRAPHIC DESIGNER

DEVIN DEVINE, ASSISTANT EDITOR

JILL KOLONGOWSKI, MANUSCRIPT COPY EDITOR

JAMES SULLIVAN, ASSISTANT EDITOR

"We like to think of it as parallel to what we know,
Only bigger. One man against the authorities.
Or one man against a city of zombies."

"My God, It's Full of Stars," TRACY K. SMITH

"Once they were dead, and after that they were called
back to life again."

"Tell My Horse," ZORA NEALE HURSTON

Contents

Strange Flowers

i

American Monster

Thursday, I am born,
of the white glove's careless C-section, twilight
of the gods who couldn't give my mother
more time, instead unspooled her innards,
attempted anthropomancy, divined her son
a serpent circling the world. My birth
paradoxical, of the myth that this world has
a beginning, an end. To the doctors, my body
grows suspiciously quick. On the block, my head
looms above the branches. Bewitched
by Mercedes, I lose her basketball bet, wear
the pink skirt, pretend rebus, double-headed beast.
Society strikes first. An officer accuses me of looming
over fences. The old heads accuse me of being sweet.
I open my mouth & four canines. I open my mouth
& the cujo's bat-bitten. I open my mouth & Fenrir's
wild gnawing the hand that feeds. It is the forgotten
eighth day that something inside me dies inside
of my own mouth and putrefaction sets in. Mourning,
I don black jeans, black hoodie, black menis.
A white man crosses the street when he sees: me,
maggots, Muspell, multiple-choices in the form
of one question. What follows? What follows.

Alternate Histories of the Exquisite Corpse

after A Brief History of Cyborgs by Franny Choi

A red giant collapses into a neutron star. Its strange matter escapes
to convert all other kinds into an ideal state—Or

The Surrealists create absurd creatures: swans reflecting elephants,
evening spiders, the dream and real merged into supra—Or

An ancestor of the hog nose snake discovers, if pretending to be a cobra
doesn't work, to lie on the ground and play dead—Or

When the police leave after the traffic stop, I get up from that nadir, live
long enough to be buried with gray hair in a beautiful suit—Or

The word opossum is derived from an Algonquian phrase meaning
"white animal" e.g. *The white animal will play dead to escape a threat,
can turn cannibalistic in captivity*—Or

I am terrified of the idea of white supremacy in Black face. Afraid that Jim
Crow will come back even after it has appeared to die—Or

In a dream gone awry I am chased by people who have passed. When
they catch me, I open my eyes to lucid, respawn as if in a game—Or

The rules of the Exquisite Corpse game are the following: players write in turn on a sheet of paper, fold it to conceal part of the writing, and then pass it to the next player for a further contribution—Or

After Zora Neale Hurston's work in "Tell My Horse," Harvard scientist Wade Davis claims a person can make a zombie by adding certain chemicals to a body. His findings are castigated for being erroneous—Or

If you repeat a lie long enough, it becomes the truth—Or

The word "zombi"— first appeared without the "e" in a short story called "The Unknown Painter" in 1838. In the story, an African slave owned by a Spanish painter proclaims that a "zombi" goes in at night to make beautiful paintings, but no one believes him—Or

I paint portraits of white people only for the white person to receive most of the credit. When I tell people what I've seen, no one believes me—Or

In the late 2000s the zombie was romanticized as a companion for the film's hero. They were substitutes for the disenfranchised, the relationship between zombie and human an analogy for the destruction of convention—Or

Most of the white people I know have in some way said, you are so warm, so warm and then *I hate my neighborhood so full of summer*—Or

After the fungus Ophiocordyceps unilateralis has infected an ant, a stalk stretches from the back of the dead insect head like a solid stream of blood—Or

I don't paint portraits of Black people because they don't tell the whole story. Instead, I make films of them breaking down doors after being locked out of a beautiful southern gothic. Sometimes, I'm still accused of editing in the part when they are mistaken for a something else and shot—Or

If you repeat a lie long enough, it becomes the end—Or

(un)dead

Does anyone else, while watching
the video of the cop shooting the black
man / boy / person on the internet

pause the video right before it ends?
I do—It doesn't matter if it's the one
with Tamir or Oscar.

Sometimes, right before it gets to the end
I'll stop it, then hit rewind—It's always bizarre
witnessing the body rise and the cop

retreat, climb back into their car
before fleeing in reverse. Likewise, it is
strangely beautiful to see the snow

(un)red as the bullet exits the (un)dead
body and return into the barrel's black,
the boy / man / person now standing,

walking. Does anyone else shed
a tear, a smile? Is it just me?

Self-portrait of the artist as a *Zombie*

But then again, there's the painting, the graffiti of a zombie in black acrylic on an abandoned building by the old home along with the phrase, *Still Alive*—I used to jog by its form-mirroring-function, its derelict branded on derelict, its meta slowly renovated, transformed from an empty shell into a nest for bees,

a brewery with honey, nectar, the tagged zombie painted over with white. But still within, the folks leering as I ran toward home: my mother not knowing if I would return alive in that city, that country, that time, another kind of ruin, threatening to consume me if I stop— In one draft, I do and the abandoned

building turns me into an abandoned building filled with insects—And yet, in the final frame—Winter, a boy who looks like me is standing in the doorway, while a woman who resembles my mother jerks her hand away from his face as it returns to her—Still alive, but cold.

Still Life: Roses in a Makeshift Vase

Sometimes
    a lover just wants you
    to bring them
a dying thing—

    And so, I find myself
        at the bus stop, on Valentine's Day,
        in Michigan where the winter wind
        is killing me, slow enough that I can
    make it to the store before it does me in—

        Earlier that day, a friend had sent a text about
    how in ancient times on this special occasion

Romans would kill a goat
    and use the still wet skin as a whip
    for striking women
in order to boost their fertility—

Sometimes
    a woman wants this, these:
    A dead thing / To be struck / To be covered in the blood

Often

       a man does too—But on that evening
       it is a woman who stands before me—As I hold
       a bouquet behind my back

    the rubies of which I reveal to the beaming
light of her face its florets like brilliant blades
its stems bursting forth with red sickle shapes.

No vase.
She sets the dozen in a coffee pot
       leaves them to brew beneath the kitchen's fluorescent bulb
             their organic glow building on vermillion edges,

a half-life, an undead beauty like radioactive waves outstretched
penetrating
       like x-rays—I feel a pang in my chest
       and then a raindrop on my right hand—
       Looking, I see a tiny prick and rose blossom
where a thorn must have bitten in.

I say nothing—
       By then, she has made her way
       to the couch and motions for me to join.
And because

sometimes,

a lover wants you

to bring them a dying thing,

I shuffle myself over to her

      and kiss her, once more—once more

On Family

Claim that Family is everything: vamp,
        spook sitting by the front door, on Boo
n' nem grave, denizens of Ante-Purgatory,
        the excommunicated—On

March 3, 1956, my mother's father departs Haiti,
        bids *au revoir* to Tonton Macoutes,
but also his mother. The list of dead
        include his cousins unable to escape—On

the orders of a President, my father wanders
        Kuwait in withdrawal. Fields of fescue
colorless compared to what follows him—
        When she heard what he was on

my aunt said, *Si Bondye vie,*
        or *we are all made in God's image.*
Hebrews 11:1, "Now faith is being sure
        of what we hope for." On and On,

our family tree's gigantic, hundred handedness.
        Our mother tongues grew
Creole, English vernacular on one branch
        as Erykah Badu played in the background—On

the guys, my cousin J. dipped out the crib

      for the corner's hustle, the caress of a solid crew.

When prison-swallowed inked a bestiary on his skin,

      a winged animism flashing neon.

Generally, my cousins Walter Dean Myers monstrous,

      charged when white folk cross avenues

to avoid their undying. If recruited for a Theomachy

      no god would escape—On

everything, the men in my family go

      where morning dew is nectar to their feet. A few

were never men, the divine a spectrum granting

      their feminine ease—"Godson

bring that photo album out the attic!"

      Not every member has a framed picture in the living room.

A shoe box labeled, [Birdsong] collects dust.

      An extant history waits years for admission.

I feel most like a zombie after consuming a cocktail

two parts dark rum, one part OJ,
a splash of grenadine, orange slice—
I feel most like a zombie when consuming
a leg from Popeyes, chicken fried rice,
lip grease smear, that one episode of
Key & Peele where the ghouls flee from them
wide eyed, hustle over a wooden fence.
I be their coal by the grill, their unbothered
in the backyard. A walking infomercial,
I bear a bag of trash and call it Glad,
limp on a twisted ankle that will never heal.

I feel most like a zombie when I see red and blue lights,
in the rear view, when I hear *hands up*!
I am most like a zombie when I am out in the street
after they have killed another one of us.
By us, I mean a second cousin once removed.
By us, I mean, we who spirited here in droves,
we who moan death rattle, build a bass
that could break stained glass.
Our state has trouble separating from our church,
so I sing "Stomp," chew a piece of Christ flesh,

drink his blood with a slice of cucumber outside
    a courthouse with the jurors they refused.

I feel most like a zombie waking up to a hangover,
    my Ti bon ange buzzing in my pocket.
One text leads, *I want to be Most Honorable Judge,*
    Mystical Black . . . another reads, *Let me know*
when you get home safe. I don't respond with words.
I am well beyond words now.
    I feel most human when surrounded by people
who are only there in spirit. I feel most human
    when they pull my water from the ground, pour me
into a *tej*: two parts water, one part honey.
    I feel most human when they hold the white wine,
add some Barbancourt, small saucepan, low flame—
    When the stirring has stopped, when the strainer
has given its last drop, I offer them something to drink.

ii

White Zombie

—after the 1933 film White Zombie starring Bela Lugosi

you do not stop at tree limbs
creeping into cinereal, palm roots
in the path of darkness.

you drive into the midst
of Black people burying their loved one
in the middle of the road,

this path taking you past the parish
to the plantation to be married,
king, queen, to be marred not in the cards.

you drink the poison yet can taste only sweetness.
you, the most dangerous type of zombie there is.
you say nothing, play Liszt on the piano.

you cannot hear your lover saying,
rather you be dead than in the hands of natives,
only them calling you in the middle of

the nightmare you stir from.
& you think have been cured,
what your master means when he toasts,

to the future   a dream you outlive.

you keep on keeping on,

a hard figure beneath a white veil

waiting for a hand.

you do not know you are a zombie yet.

right now, you are in love.

History of Dementia

My nana forgets the time I brought home a soccer plaque / My
crooked smile as she held it is lost / along with the dazzled taxi driver
eyeing her in the rearview / Her brain holds back Cabaret's blue
The mountains, the coup, all forgotten in her plaques / When I caught
the croup at six, she gave me medicine that killed the fever in the old
way, this night disappeared in a prion / Plaque such an ugly word:
plaqueplaqueplaqueplaqueplaque / Repeating, it becomes easy to confuse
with *plague* / Too much of the illness and she forgets how she admires
Rory Flack, her ice skating, silver, her backflip / Too much and she
knocks the soccer plaque out of my hands and snaps at her daughter,
the black spots on her teeth shining as she snarls at us / A biofilm's
breadth from woundedness, we leave the hospital / My mom acts as if
she is fine, but I know she's not, know that nana's plaques, her tangles,
are starting to get to her, hijack her mother, rot enamel / Her mother
who, close to the end says, *pitit gason*, the bronze plaques of her irises
shimmering briefly before becoming as sharp as a tack / *Pierre?* she
asks, half-remembering a lover's shadow / shine

Like

preposition. 1: similar to: Because there has to be an easier way of knowing, than knowing, *like* reading the Times or the bones, *like* distant sirens that sound *like* Black women screaming or sopranos singing into the night. Because there must be a better way of understanding than experiencing—*like*. So when you ask what it is similar to, the answer is close enough. It is *like* the beat cops I saw turned shades chasing down black boys in Michigan, *like* if you can't join them beat them, *like* a feverish Indiana night, a horde glittered with sweat ready to lynch two men and feast their eyes, *like* locusts swarming a field of grain as gold as youth. It is *like* the waters of hurricane Harvey subsuming Houston streets, *like* wildfires consuming homes in California, the shadows of prisoners stretching before the eyes, *like* a hard way to realize there aren't enough fire fighters. Otherwise, it is *like* an epidemic, opioid, oblique, *like* a flash mob but the dance is deportation, but a trans woman in Dallas is the vehicle they attempt to tip, *like* a scale, *like* Russian bots peddling misinformation until one becomes a hit, goes viral, each shared clip garnering another *like*.

Still Life: In the Field Where My Brother Died

She paints him false. His body, factory floor
perfect. Not aflame in that field. Not the chassis
warped like wax. Instead, the Adopt-A-Highway
sign with its [*in memory of*] in linseed oil, the sky
behind as blue as his eyes watching over, the maple trees

beneath, brown as his brunette at the foothill's base
washed white, eloping with that gentle slope and looking dead
in Winter's embrace, but not. The hay poking
out of the thin sheet of snow gold like his hair
the one time he went blonde. She shows not the blood

but the barn in lieu, a hard-earned cardinal red in the background,
adds into the middle ground, a view—The house
he moved in with his brother, green as the grass on
the other side—She knows no one can see the interior,
imagines: a ceiling the color of jaundice, beige carpets

stained with cherry cola, a dead cat melted into the heater,
against a wall that turned a waterfall of spaghetti
and wept until she painted it over with concrete.
In the foreground, he stands smiling with a fish
in his hand, his pink finger a worm hooking the poor thing

by its gills. In reality it was a muskie but she makes it
a lake sturgeon and easier on the eyes—She paints him
tactile, enduring, the Adopt-A-Highway sign sprouting
from the dirt, a rack of color refracting white light into
rainbow—No one sees the drafts, the hours of courtroom

sketches, the balled up, crumpled, half-finished likenesses.
No one sees the white-knuckle grip, the figure that was
almost added to that bean field. She unpaints them true,
a shadow, half-sketch, half mercy. When she colors in
the tattoos it is love, not forgiveness.

Fever

A frenzy—like one of those nights before Fahrenheit
when the heat was immeasurable. Yes then, the bedroom

held me shaking in its black body, its radiation not like,
but is, is the head split but no goddess leaking out,

no beads of sweat but a boiling, but oceans of ache,
but waves of muscle roiling beneath flush skin, a fervor

fierce enough to make the light go out from behind the eyes,
turn a laughing child into a vegetable, swell a tongue into

a raspberry, lymph nodes so large they could swallow
man, memory, mother bringing water in a cup. What purple plastic?

What anthropomorphic duck? What water could endure
as the forest of me turned Sahara Desert, as my animal became

a pet stranded in a sedan, without air conditioning, begging for rain?
Forget forgetfulness, I was a dune that believed it could walk

to the bathroom, then a delirious decaliter of sand poured into
a white tub, coffin cold. I tried looking in the mirror,

but it remained a window leading into night,
tried peeking out the glass only to see my reflection staring

at two moons, blush round each cheek, cheek,
four heads lavender bloom, a third eye the color of dawn,

I, I, I, seeping from the brow's lipid envelope,
tongues outside the mouths hotter than dog days,

canines in the street, beneath green magnolia leaves,
in their ferment, the fever breaking. I fell dead asleep—

woke to a songbird's solfège. That day,
a child I touched briefly fell, hotter than a tear

on a summer sidewalk, and was gone so quick, *so*

American Realism

In college, to pay for books, I worked
at an art gallery that featured "American Realism."
At first the owner insisted I work for free
but paid me when I insisted.

I straightened frames and wrote Facebook posts
on how "Cindy House's wetland landscape delights
the senses with intricate detail over a larger canvas.
Her frame nothing less than a portal."

During breaks, I delighted in a portal of my own:
House of Cards, *The Walking Dead*. My favorite character,
a Black woman named Michonne who walked
the apocalyptic wielding a samurai sword.

The longer I watched her, the more
her character made its way into my gallery.
I began seeing her in Andrew Wyeth's *Granary and Mill*
scavenging for blond grain, in *Graffiti*,

Blond, blending in to survive. Soon, in all the paintings,
her portrait, her passing, her performance—
I wondered, as she strolled through a field holding
two men in chains, if her performance was

feminist or womanist? When she used
severed limbs in a found object sculpture
spelling out "GO BACK," did she mean
spatially or temporally? In the giclée

of her talking to the blade like a long-lost lover,
was the conversation a coping mechanism?
Did the blade, removed from her grasp,
resume its role as a phallic symbol?

When the governor   she gouged out
his right eye and severed his left hand
but didn't kill. His death ultimately came
at Lily's white hand. Was this a collaboration?

And still, I wondered how I was meant to consume
this piece without America as a context?
After all, wasn't this a post-apocalyptic world,
wasn't her art a commentary on the death

of a country itself—And yet
the next day that country had risen. Exhibition day
people streamed in and the owner had me serve
white wine. There was no red wine because

once someone had spilled it, sullying the white marble.
There was a photograph for sale titled

Ebony that resembled her before everything fell to pieces.
In it she was full, hoop earring,

black background, chromogenic print. No one bought it.

The state of Florida interviews the "The Miami Zombie"

F: What finds you on the MacArthur Causeway?
R: A broke down caprice. A car that was never
going nowhere.

F: How hot would you say it is?
R: Fifth circle Fahrenheit and humid. This always happens
by the way. Something breaking, right when I'm on the way
somewhere—And, here they go again.

F: Who?
R: The tune of traffic: Sonata, Impala, Ram.

F: Who are you wearing?
R: Sacred skin. My shirt a straitjacket I sweated out of.

F: If you were a car would you be an Impala or a Ram?
R: I'd be a caprice, plum or mauve, royal. Revelation 1:6 says,
"Christ has made us kings and priests."

F: Are you armed?
R: I've got two testaments with me, clutched and bundled
in my sweat. Dog-eared pages slipping from my grasp,
to gravel, but in me anyway: stomach, spleen, Septuagint

as the window glass's glint stands in for water on which
my faith can walk. So, I unlace my shoes.

F: What kind of vehicle are you?
R: Ram, caught in a bush,
burnt offering in place of someone's son.

F: Do you think it will rain?
R: A flood on account of my blackity,
black, my skin's Egyptian knowledge.
Ancient ascetics would strip down,
wade in wilderness.

F: When did you meet the man in the wilderness?
R: The devil met me in the city of big water,
at the lowest point said, "If you the son
of God, fly to the top."

F: What day was it?
R: Saturday. But he kept calling me Monday, Monday,
Monday. I knew he meant, moon cricket,
Day of the Moon. Concealed within his code,
a celestial body.

F: Did you know him?
R: Barely. He asked for the time. I didn't have a watch.
There was nothing but his palms, his face's
physiognomy. I saw the future, his gaze, his life

line short. His left eye called me a Monday,
threatened damnation, so I cut it out.

F: What future did you see?
R: A time when all I had was my hands.
In a way, I was always an understudy to it,
my dad breaking the bathroom door neatly,
how the hinges barely bent, popped, a single
red dent, a rose on his fist.

F: What future did you see?
R: A college boy reframing the sin, handsome as a waxing gibbous.
For him, a stun gun, for him, a kick to the head, for him,
don't shoot and *preternatural strength*, compliments to his bear-like
scalping the husband's face, a splitting of the veil of the temple
above the eyebrow, the deputies entering the house like wise men
bearing gifts.

F: What future did you see?
R: What every almanac knows, the Monday, Monday, Monday,
Monday of each month, the festival of the hightide,
the ceremony of the eclipse.

The Brooms

after One Impression *by Yona Harvey*

They insist that he is peering down on us from heaven
and yet, I can't help but notice, standing at the front of
the church we are actually staring down at him, comely
in a casket's cocoon, childlike in a black suit—

As we take our seats the pastor drips stoicism from his lips.
Apparently feeling himself, he tries to go two for one on souls
for God, does an altar call and gets mine. My cousin having just
died, I wasn't taking any chances with death that day. Though

after the funeral it isn't long before I have seller's remorse,
and then, it is a long time until I feel like buying into anything again—
If we had still been in the old country, there wouldn't have been a funeral.
Instead, a symbolic grave, instead a burying up to the neck

in superstitious earth, the *zombi* being his disease, the *zombi* being
the hearse tricked into remaining while my cousin is freed,
pulled from the dirt like a stalk of bunchgrass, no rootedness,
but a harvest of him, a buying of his beige, his brownish-purple

back from the dead, from the spirit of the recently dust—
And yet, my family did not go late at night to the intersection

of two roads, to cut a check, make payment. My cousin
did not lie on top of the tomb, but inside, unable to hear;

no healer to sweep his body with a broom, to brush away
the negative, no bristles moving x, x, x to mark him as
clean, cleansed— And so, to keep the faith, I tell myself
that in rooms all across this land; across this world

there are brooms, which the grieving, hopeful use to sweep *t, t, t,*
like little crosses, *c, c, c* like crescent moons, stars of all stripes
in that internal place made pristine, as a sigil, sign, ritual, just in case
someone is looking.

The Deer

The algorithm took us round
        a whole other way, the driver said
as we pulled up to the apartment.
        It was my friend's birthday.
I hugged her in the room with pink walls,
        full of smiles, a pot of coffee
brewing as we waited for brunch—
        Daydreaming, my mind flickered
through my to-do list: laundry, dishes,
        the undead deer poem,
I was so excited to write.
        I was so excited to invoke
the chronic wasting disease,
        echo, *Eocene*, *Epoch*,
render a buck head
        with lowered antlers
wandered aimless from
        a dry ravine, the bovine
and vine, the rifle
        a Remington Model 700,
the prion protein misfold
        camouflaged in the prey
like a hunter. Only when cooked
        would the venison turn,

the opposite of a song, a scream—

But then, it was time to eat and drink.
The blinds were opened. Daylight poured in

like mimosa into a glass and we began to speak
about this, that, and the other. Eventually

we got on the topic of the town.
People had been feeding the deer too much,

and they'd started coming around more,
fearing the human touch less. Something

had to be done—A few residents had
already polished their guns, discussed

a small cull. Some of the more liberal suggested
an alternative—In the lull that followed

a man was hired to tranq bulls,
sterilize them beneath starlight,

streetlamp. How it is that a child
witnessed the act at night is unclear,

and yet, it leered at them, how effortlessly
what is internal can become apparent.

It was agreed that the deer, once asleep,
would be moved to a high school gym

where they'd begin a new life
in the home of the Pioneers,

a group of concerned moms
raising money to buy yoga mats for them

to rest on once the procedure was done—
Everyone at the party knew

what a gym looked like,
and yet, none of us could imagine
what poses they did in the dark.

iii

Zorapocalypse: An Interview with *Tell My Horse* by Zora Neale Hurston

Q: Would you say a part of the author lies in their book?

A: A book is often the opposite of a barracoon.

Q: As brother of Barracoon: The Story of the Last "Black Cargo," what would you say about the present-day condition of the family?

A: We are like an eternal field hand to it. From it we take our orders and never fatigue.

Q: When you say "it" what exactly do you mean?

A: I mean, the disappeared woman is found years later mindless, that the refugees marched past the houses where they once lived won't remember.

Q: Being familiar with the zombie in Haiti, what do you make of the genre of the zombie apocalypse?

A: When I hear apocalypse, I hear revelation. When I hear zombies, I hear Gonaïves rebellion, critical mass marching in Georgia, midnight habeas corpus.

Q: What kind of revelation do you hear?

A: Ayibobo and Amen from Pittsburgh to Paris. A revolution by any other name.

Q: How does this revolution begin?

A: Patient zero then, zeptoseconds later, a Big Bang.

Q: Does this revolution mean the end of slavery?

A: It means a people large enough for their own zodiac. The Rebirth of a Nation. A parthenogenesis. A Black Joan of Arc.

Q: Speaking of Joan of Arc, Zora certainly looks the part in this photo. What can you tell us about it?

A: The light lipsticked her lucent, rattle in her left hand heavier than you thought it could be, the robes soft as shadow, the *hountar* black synesthesia, mother, drum, mama drum.

Q: What did the drums sound like?

A: Erzulie, red eyes of loss
   Black bull, Petro Flame-eyed moth
   Shadows beat to quick the drum
   White robes dipped in evening's rum
   Cochon gris: The silver pig
   Eat, The Rich. *Eat the rich,*
   Colloquial of the poor
   Quartz cuvette by the front door
   Eminence of the Black Stone
   Dog corpse on the altar, key
   Infant by the cotton tree
   Masks meet men where demons seep
   Horns of cows and goats beseech
   Speckled bird in the crossroad.

Q: You certainly don't hear that in the States do you?

A: If the bones in Léogâne were quiet, if the disciples in Louisville were silent, we would hear it from the stones.

Q: In Chapter 17 a lot of time is spent interviewing Dr. Reser, a white man, but what can you tell me about the drum player you call Cicerone?

A: He knows the island like the back of his hand, knows the mandrake buried in its heart, pale roots hemming the houngan's art, the animal they try to get it out. He has seen the men in trees plying secret societies, could've foretold timberland stretching through our own time; that story within a story, Dragon tattoo on the white sailor's left arm, a snake before it was an egg; before it was an egg, a small Black thing, wet jewel in the sand.

Q: Then why focus on the Doctor?

A: It's not that the Doctor knows the island better. The outsiders come because he explains it in a way they can understand: Shango, Thor. Guédé, Charon, wet warm dark of the island, warm wet dusk in the Ozarks, Lapland rinsed in summer heat, if flashed before foreign eyes not quite Pont Beudet but close enough. The Doctor is not one of them but close, a tempest, or rather a tempest brought him there. The tourists listen to him the as if it would free them, pay no mind to Brother Bouki, Ti Malice in the bush, Cicerone who they do not call Caliban or Ariel, but say words like *magic, shaggy,* things like, *when he plays the drums he is not one of us.*

Q: So it's a question of audience?

A: To the Other, English is the language of the Other.

Q: That's fascinating. Looking back would you say you were an outsider?
A: English. English. English. English.

Q: How do we as outsiders get closer to the truth of a place?
A: By going. And then, by carrying it with us.

Q: How do we carry it with us?
A: Like a horse carries Guedé.

Q: And how is that?
A: If not careful, like glue. Done proper, déjà vu.

First Person Plural

We / not a boat people / rather / water

undammed / a waiting hurricane / *ADAM*

ADAMADAM / bursting / sons & daughters

pouring over the walls / the best laid plans

Ready or not / re:Fugees / No calm eye /

we / wind whipping wasp nests under the eaves—

No warning / No breeze / Our team with no I

teeming across horizons like the eve

Nou / a new storm / each drop bearing a name

Evens / Fabienne / Junior / Widelene

& negotiating with that same / same

on shore / those amber waves of grain—

Cousin / what category of longing is this

to have brought us so far from genesis?

Future of Dementia

Because *first permanent non-Indigenous settler* doesn't have the same ring to it, Jean Baptiste Point du Sable is known as Chicago's founder, his trading post a kiss to the river's mouth. I wonder in all his years battling blizzards, dreaming of south, could he have foreseen a black belt grown wide, Bronzeville settled with brown, my mother, her second-generation summering?

In Morgan Park the post white flight blacks assumed all roles in the community: doctor, lawyer, teacher. Lessons that didn't require literacy assigned to children. It was they who waited for winter, first snow heaped right below freezing point, brought gloves, dexterous fingers to pack powder into artificial sintering, arc orbs alee brick bungalows to quietly break apart   across her back, chest, face   calls of *darky, jungle,* exploding around the ears   Years and she   would   never forget,   would love snow in free fall, always fear it in that shape

inking internal inkling   A T C G   old   alphabet   made

auspicious   Suspicious   my mother did not teach me   Creole

I picked up another tongue, cold hard fact off the ground   could

hold that ivory in my palm easily as an elephant tusk   crush and

sculpt   and sling into navy blue   ski masks unblinking curve ball

a chalky globe   to land above   the brow like an eraser blow on a chalkboard   & baptize not just people

Practicing   I'd throw the white at objects: car   windshields

bare bark   trees   indistinguishable without their leaves

getting warmer   I'd hurl the language at stop signs   watch

the red diminish   even the pearl of the lettering unable to stand up

to the snow

The Tourist

My red gingham print and khaki slacks do not fool immigration,
who name the dark tidal pool of my hair and must now see proof
of the conference at the local college—I purchase adapter, adapt
to the city's reversed intersections, the car's swerving almost.

A tourist lost in a maze of Georgian homes, Maman Brigit
on the General Post Office, the silent triumph of Easter
Sunday's Uprising, that liberated republic with wealth for granite
wreaths. In the hostel, a Black man from the Netherlands gushes

European dream, as if no one had told him of this hostile we live in.
At the conference, a confluence of recessions, ghost houses in the
countryside, why to this day an anti-humanist communion, a collective
crimson sings "Zombie" like The Cranberries—In Dublin 1, before

the dissolution, a conference of Limerick fans in super blue.
I black eye stick out, make a molt of money, cop a cream shirt dotted
with small black ships. We set our armada for Temple Bar,
my sole Black friend in the city in tow as Mr. Brightside turns saints

into seas. River gods carved into the wall imbibe in this light
and we drink until it is Sunday again—I pay a visit to the James Joyce
museum where they act as if he has risen, then St. Stephens Green, the
black bust of a friend who died in war. My new friend would have said,

he, dead, dead, noted the black bust wanted to be *junior partner,* or *sure they "friends,"* alluded to the link between men in Thailand bathhouses—
Speaking for himself the Black bust says, *poet,* says, *And for the secret Scripture of the poor.* More softly, he sighs, *At some point your friends can't . . .*

At some point, no one is going to hold your hand...I live sometimes in
that moment on the plane during takeoff, when, from above, the country
looks like it could be the past or future of any country, all that green
stretching endless. This time I wear a different kind of fatigue—

When I return home, all the cars are going the wrong way.

The Atlanta Child Murderer on playing *Black Ops*

It was a game he used to play on weekends / He still remembers the tutorial / training in the woods / how to secure a perimeter / engage the enemy / how to clear a room / how to shoot / glock / remington / winchester / how to kill with a knife / with his bare hands cross / palm strike / rear chokehold / When he felt / he felt the body go limp / knew he had passed the test / The field was different / He didn't feel like himself / himself / said it felt like he was watching someone else / like watching an avatar / Simon says / Someone else had the controller / control / He wasn't the one that actually did it / He wasn't the one who drove the car / the one who cleared the room / the one who dropped the body off the bridge / He had the controller but didn't have control / He said / he said / it was for country / He said / we were just doing what other boys / men / what other soldiers were doing around the world / When we went online / when we heard the call / we fought the enemy / foreign / domestic / soldiers at first / until we cleared a room / human at first / until we went further / deeper in that darkness / in that neck of the woods / those things weren't human / were spooks / bogeys / monsters / dropshot / dropshot / We had orders to clear them from that space / to keep them from spreading / in Georgia / night missions / night vision / They don't tell you about all the colors / bursts of drake's neck green / falu red / labrador blue / scarlet / They don't tell you about the light in their eyes / It seemed to double / triple / there was no end to it

The Z----- Goes to Therapy

My therapist tells me I have an adjustment disorder,
a maladaptive response to a psychosocial stressor.
She says I have difficulty coping, doesn't say what
she thinks the stressor might be—As I sit and wait
for my lemon ginger tea to steep, we talk about
how I've been more comfortable with routine lately:
coffee shop consume, chipotle, red mild carnitas,
in solitude a porn consommé. She says the signs
can include: Sagittarius descending, sadness, desperation,
crying spells, suicidal thoughts. I tell her for me it's mostly
a walking anxious, the sky overcast but never rain, feeling
always on, going always, apartment on my back, $750
for a clogged sink. I tell her how I've been thinking that
I've been in this state a while and so this world a while now.
Been in it so long my parents have divorced twice, so long
the microaggressions have piled up into their own mountain—
I tell my therapist the microaggressions don't make me mad
anymore, just paranoid. I tell her what I think my doctor thinks,
that if I'm poked with a needle I won't feel the pain, yet act
as if I do. I know it doesn't make sense. I put my lips to the tea
and burn my tongue. It hurts, but I don't say anything—
There are blood oranges on the side table in a blue bowl.
I remove the skin on one, eat it to soothe the sting,
put another in my coat for later. Later, I will look up

adjustment disorders online. The source I find will suggest
it serves only as a non-stigmatizing label, a diagnosis
for insurance coverage. Later, I will forget about
the orange in my coat pocket and it will go bad.

Black Zombi

I am everywhere the dark touches

     N----- brown, pupil of the eye, winking sclera.

I open envelopes of reality as I walk

     brilliant moth blade through suburbia.

I stand, a stamp in its corner,

     America forever, arrived a-

     lone wolf, sanctioned super-

     predator. In the now,

     in the, it is what it is,

     twilight, hard snow shining on the hill,

     black ice leading to imported stone,

     wisps of smoke weaving from chimney

     through bare branches.

I gaze into heavenly mansions.

I peek into the houses

     for something lit to steal,

     window shop as the doors hold strong.

     The locks hold strong,

     yet what is precious rushes out the windows,

     stainless steel, marble on fleek,

     mahogany, high-definition foyers

     lit from an arc lamp's off-white wish.

They wouldn't believe me if I said,

     In the highest window

someone playing Haunted House.
Mickey Mouse playing piano
to appease skeletons.
But, it is what it is, the truth
on grandma's grave.
My own grave keeps
changing location depending
on the time of my arrival.
I am everytime, crossing the border
into the land of the un-
afraid, the daemon they don't know
they know.
The couple approaching me
on sidewalk believes in beauty borne by
distance, the frozen pine, the half-moon's tryst
with dark greenery.
I camouflage then
I background fade, invisible to them
in the boundary, the distance dying
down, and making our way
from different places
to different places, we all morph
into that place by the park,
the baying dog, the rabbit in shadow.
Nobody can get rid of,
this space we have become.
No one owns this.

Roleplaying

I am the cursor's scrolling ionic column
shifting into arrow, white-gloved hand.
you are the hot single in my area seeking,

the porn site's A-Z: ass, ebony, oral,
zombie, the last category I expect to find.
I am for the first time how others view

pornography, a thing bereft of beauty,
a decadent decay. you are the Live Jasmine
pop-up framed in scarlet, the woman

waking in a bed, queen-sized. I am your
pale partner, neck wound and eye shadow,
equally no one special, the director's

offscreen, a groan of pleasure, a lustful
lunge. you are the script's command, Asa
Akira's arch, a bare neck submitting yes

after yes, after yes. We be this clip edited
for mass consumption, this stroke and pant
and ministry of the switched position,

of doggie style's migration to missionary.
you, black hair whipping back and forth,
a command, *look at me*. Me, a longing gaze.

Me, both hot single seeking, supple.
You, the strange light in your own eyes,
the bite of my waiting neck. Me, the arch,

the mouth begging, *right there*, your perfume,
your glitter. You, direction and demand,
lips asserting Abaddon. Me, averted eyes,

a sigh, a safe word unspoken.

Morning of the Living Dead

—after "Dinosaurs in the Hood" by Danez Smith, "The Condition of Black Life Is One of Mourning" by Claudia Rankine & Night of the Living Dead *by George Romero*

After the critically acclaimed cult

Classic: starring a Black girl

From Chicago, named *Chicago*,

Her pet crow named *Gem*.

A scene of them traveling

With *Queen* and *Ocean*

During day to show

How mourning is different

From grief. Because of grief

All allies wear black,

Gather in public spaces at night

Despite the lumbering threat,

Armed men in the countryside.

Cut to cityscape. Cut to

Monsters milling like sheep.

Extended action sequence:

Queen with a staff,

Queen with kung-fu,

Ocean driving.

Forty-seven extras cast

From the Potomac Gardens,

Black bandana charge—
Climax: *Chicago* bitten,
Ocean injured, red oil spill.
Scene in which a Black woman discovers
The cure. Scene with a Black woman
Who been found the cure, last century,
Last week, last second.
We want their eyes to open,
Want a benediction
From DC's brown mayor.
We want this sequel to be
As good as, if not better than
The original.
Want no critics saying
It is unrealistic
Everyone lives.

iv

Black Summer

Episode 1:

Exterior: The future looks bright when I shake the hand, when I get the job. I have a job so I think I can't be killed. If I'm killed who will put on the striped polo, who will iron the khaki slacks in the soft blue glow of morning? In the interview I don't mention my carlessness, the city closing the main train to our part of town. My parents warn me not to take the bus, mutter something, *southside, serpent.* But, they weren't there at the interview in the Heliopolis, when asked about a time I overcame an obstacle, the answer I did not give. And yes, I want this job. And yes, I will do what is required. And no, I won't be late, and yes, I need to know if I have what it takes to earn a living in this world. So I lie so well that they never find out, and I brush my hair, and the sun was shining when I left.

Episode 2:

Exterior: There is a silver lining in being late, a silver lining in the headless gargoyle stooping on the building overlooking the bus stop, silver lining in the old neighbors having spirited his head away during their white flight. I fly now down the street, *shoe, shoe, shoe, shoe,* bull and 98 Jordan sprinting for the championship shot against the jazz of rain and distant thunder, sprinting like my livelihood depends on this hunger, this hustle, this two-block chase of timely folk. When the doors open the driver says *Peace god,* says *His airness.* Exterior: This is my training day. On some silent G shit, homie in the back with the star tattoo schools me, says *be cool.* We sit with the AC on high, our faces like stone.

Episode 3:

Exterior: My employment center gig begetting more jobs. I have two jobs now, am job rich. From job #1 on the Southside, I travel to job #2 downtown, down Throop street's troop laden toward the number 9 bus. I wait at the intersection of 79th and Ashland thumbing sweat beads as a rosary for silent prayers. After three Apostles Creeds a Black boy answers. He tries to shake me up like I am unemployed or in his line of business or a friend or an enemy or he just wants to touch. His fingers linger limp in the air, poised to strike. I stare at his hand, a bouquet flush with thorns. If I shake it we are blood, if I shake it there will be blood.

Episode 4:

Exterior: I lie for a living, I say I am somewhere I am not, allude I am someone who does not exist. I, lie of omission. I do not exist for a living. It pays well, a beautiful scam. I work the fourth of July, forfeit my independence, the corded phone a snake to my ear whispering of capital's fruit. A customer is angry that I didn't know the height he almost fell would have killed him. I've never been to the property, am unable to see the gap, the distance. He hangs up, the dial tone bleeding out into silence. I go on lunch. On my newsfeed a <u>hunger strike begins in California</u>, 29,000 inmates protesting solitary confinement practices. I eat lunch alone in a windowless room. Tonight, they will paint the sky with strange flowers—

Episode 5:

Exterior: There's sweat dripping down the brown neck running up the street late and air-conditioned punch card 12:01 technicality. This month I will be both. One more and they will fire me so quick I won't have time to wonder about where the term "fire" came from. I'll be the late [what's his name] disowned by work wife, work family, a bitter work father figuring everyone else late in turn. Reading Carl Sanburg's *Chicago*, again, I'll mutter, *about time you imagine a woman*. That month she will be late on bloodshed and I will see my smile in dark monitors. On the 31st I'll birth myself early bird for the first time. My coworker, the astrologer, will tell me she spies a Grand Trine in my chart, Jupiter-Saturn-Neptune, will say, *transformation is possible every day this month.*

Episode 6:

Exterior: Started from the bottom, now purgatory, now, zombie on the beat. I have mastered this role in front of a screen, now what? Behind the scenes, pressing a button to sample Ambessence Piano & Drones, pressing a button to order 26 drone strikes in Pakistan? Not yet, but what could be next. Exterior: I'm probably listening to an iPod on shuffle, not knowing what could be next on the train home: *Fucking problems, Urn, Wu Tang Forever*, a voice telling me the world is mine.

Episode 7:

Exterior: In 2013, at least 412 Chicagoans lost their lives violently, about 100 fewer than a year ago. I race anyway down the corridor that search engines have labeled dangerous. The stakes being, I've missed the bus, the stakes being, if I'm late again I will be fired. I don't know if I'm running from a certain kind of person I hate or running toward a certain kind of person I admire. I don't know what I'd do if I caught them, if I'm caught as I feel in the middle, heaving in the heavy heat. Exterior: I shudder to think what would have happened, if during that mad dash, what was inside me made it out into the world.

Episode 8:

Exterior: At job #1 the employment center helps sponsor a demonstration. We march through the street, the neighborhood they call K_____ or KingsKing. The press calls this a *peace march*. The people know it is a funeral rite. This is our priestliness at pylons, Nephthys, our wailing besetting the night-bark. We bury our David, our shepherd boy who knew no Bathbsheeba, no Jonathan. We be the moving shrine of him. We be the stuffed animals, the candles with a saint's likeness, the strange flowers. We be his photo from all angles, his monument. Because of us, he walks again into the sunset, police flanking. They chaperone us before asking us to disperse. We diffuse, what is inside us making its way out into the night.

Still Life: 'blæknəs

—after "Abstract Painting" by Ad Reinhardt

Space outside of time   shaded line of ant husks   pelican eels in
the aphotic zone   or dusk in a deciduous forest   that raccoon city
a mask for the eyes   a horizon of crow feathers   preceding home
That's so Raven   *Telephone*   like, what is a new moon if not
a black hellebore in bloom?   The queen of clubs   a book   till
the curve of spades   Till   the renege   **grrrr** in a dog's throat
ore   spots on my grandfather's liver   afro textured hair
on the barber's floor   helix shapes snaking out of the head
The contents of Louis Armstrong's horn   sheet music for Beyonce's
Halo   angels with dreads   Ebony   where the roots meet
Mississippi soil   coal as Audre Lorde's bewitching
balled into a gloved fist at the '68 Olympics   Pupils expanding after
the fire after   A starless night   how Martin Luther looked
beneath its umbra   his theses spreading like light   Redacted lines
regarding U.S. troop presence in ███████████████   Oil spilling after
the accident   Data leaking into the dark net   *Becoming*
the color of the dreams we can't remember   dreams in which
we could have done/been anything: laughter, a cry, a moan an
infectious tone   the color of silhouettes consuming
reds,   whites   Blues   If they capture you—you

Manifesto

After Audre Lorde

What to say—

The roaches were in the Cretaceous period, then Chicago,
then on the baby stroller in the kitchen, wood shadows
on white sink, winking in and out via green wallpaper.
My parents refused to acknowledge them and when they finally did,
No money for an exterminator. What to do but spray, enter each room
a one person SWAT, press down and jewel wasp paralyze, a little death
my own future could spill from. What to do but know my enemy better
then I knew myself: compound eyes, ocelli, three segment thorax.
Scientific name, *blatta.* Scientific name, *insect that shuns the light.*
Species name, *P. Americana.* Species name, *from Africa until transatlantic
slave trade, middle passage.*

What to do—

They were everywhere the light was, on coffee mugs,
in magazines, on the countertop. I was cleaning a plate.
I was cleaning a white plate and it fell. It wasn't broken,
but I threw it out anyway, in the backyard, in the middle
of winter. It was below freezing. I felt nothing, a Black boy
standing bowlegged in the backyard, dripping dishwater—

I was wrong—

They were my brothers, my sisters-in-arms,
my mother, my father, common ancestors
in brilliant bronze, far-flung descendants.
They were my babies, my beautiful babies,
unkillable even under that country's radiation.
I set the plate down, gentle in the alley.
They spilt forth beneath a broken television sky,
satellites hidden in the dark, satellites flying in the dark—
I am still alive. I am still alive.

V

Strange Flowers

In the flower beds: Begonias, Baby's breath,
Black-eyed Susans, Bland, Brown. This block
where Black lives used to live. I walk cautious

as names pop out of the ground like bulbs in spring.
A bizarre prismatic, a language of blues, lilacs
inferring the people in this house believe in beauty,

believe in what matters. This house that makes
the distinction between the flower and weeds
indiscernible. This lawn has em'. This lawn doesn't.

It shouldn't matter, yet the *science is real.*
Researchers find gardening has a similar effect
on happiness as dining out, biking. Walking,

I wonder how long these curious blossoms have
before they fall to the white burial of winter snow.
Or, if they'll emerge from earth and soil next spring,

perennial, a new name added, this diversity
a strength for property values. I suspect few
will invite the stigma inside, by the kitchen

window, in the foyer, in the bedroom,
in the bed. I imagine fewer will let them rest.

White Zombie II

Our sequel flash forwards you to hadal zone,
freezes frame on your, *You're probably wondering*
how I got here, face. Out of infinite inciting incidents
one—you spread cross hemispheres, the ocean blue
not enough boundary for you. For you, boundaries
know little resistance. you arrive eerie, imperial,
sweep like smallpox sores through Taino, a lethal lust
in your heart, your heart hard as castle, anchor.
Plot point, your sculptor sees a coat of arms, chisels
you in his likeness. your likeness popping up in all
directions: western, southern, northern gentleman.
This the setup, you postmortem ugly with no alibi,
impervious to weather. In life you speak only a few languages.
in death, everyone knows what you mean.

In death, everyone knows what you mean,
you, sprung up out the ground in Tennessee,
sundown towns still. I am born already knowing
your stock, your shadow rounding I-65,
all copies of the same man. you wish to inhabit
the minds of all who see you, place a small copy there,
devour kink and curl, anything that can't be possessed.
Midpoint, moderate mouthpieces call for barbershop debate,
as if there isn't a razor at our throats. As if there ain't

a razor at our throats, dark hands sculpt linings crisp
with arrow as signal, salons sprout battalions who brim
mirrors with secret smiling. Soon, waves and waves
and waves heed the call, cross the threshold, anointed,
protagonists chant [   ] in the street.

Protagonists chant [   ] in the street
bless the beloved even though they are buried.
Plot point, the moderates hear the chant but can't understand
the history nestled, the night air which translates our, *Hey! Hey!* to
The true number of dead is higher than what the authorities revealed.
Our *Ho! Ho!* becomes *When they killed our Charlemagne*
they made him into a scarecrow of the field. Our new language
has some variables in it, has done the math, taken note
of what is not constant. C - a = r, if C = climax, a = antagonist,
and r = resolution. Our first option is algebra's etymology,
a reunion of broken parts making both sides equal. Option 2:
Antagonist where? We trade you for a future, sink you
In the water of our bodies. Our bodies the whole time,
Sea, in a language we been known since the beginning.

Portrait of the Artist as a Spinner

I ride the unicorn, the horned horse through heaven
on earth, around the merry go round's Milky Way,
accretion disc of stars in the false sky's cresting.
In the office chair at six, a field of fluorescent bulbs.
In the office chair at 25, ballerina dreams dashed
decades before physical prime. My body what scarlet fever

and car accident couldn't kill, failed to strengthen.
My body what blasts *Still Tippin'* by Mike Jones,
pretends Slim Thug as Percocet. It is the crunk
that fights friction, the five-spoke rim of my limbs
that bears the soft tissue cyst, sickle cells, anterior
ligament sprain, collateral ligament sprain, a hernia like

a pentagram of hurt. It is the five-pointed star of
the mind that summons pain, the ghost of the Cadillac
strolling down the block, the spinner acting without
mortal engine. I begged Christ for a chromium bath,
bargained with Mephistopheles, Three 6 Mafia
to rise iridescent from the ground. The Earth replied by

rotating around a golden sun. The Moon responded
by cycling silver through omission. The body is
magical evocation, forgetting, unforgetting. How

I raced my friend on a bike to inelastic collision. How
we rose with scraped knees, doomed. A sound like
laughter as the front wheel kept going. How it keeps going.

English is [   ]

Organ Prelude

My Nana dies & there are no words, no red-letter Gospel,
no Torah, no black-inked Bhagavad-Gita.
For four days my sound sleeps behind a slab,
muted like outside the office window's thick—
My mother calls & says no words, weeps
like a widower. She weeps & I know from her
sob her ascendence to grief's throne. I hang up
the phone to absence, English an abscess
in my throat. For four days I nod athenaeum,
shake a magic 8-ball head, *no, no, ask again later.*
I mime at my boss till he gets it. My boss who
gives me bereavement or compassionate leave.

Processional

I leave by plane or by bus or by memory's unreliable,
from watershed to watershed wearing black tie,
a black veil of grief. When I get home, I shave.
When I get home, I look like a boy again, my Nana Buku
deceased, my English dead but a helium *hello*. There is
no one in our family left to do the ritual wailing
except my grandfather. He wails & English is dead again.

He wails at the front of the funeral home as we view
the [   ] His wail transports a caravan
of cars through red light intersections from repast to cathedral.
His wail & the mourners forget English, the songs, the poetry,
The Owl and the Nightingale, Beowulf's battle with
Grendel. His wail the wasteland we bury English in.

Scripture Reading & Song

The pastor reads John 14:1-3 & it is Greek to me.
A deaconess croons Ave Maria in Latin & verbicide,
& a wail in all the father's rooms. I forget having read
Elegy of Comfort, all the trees in that world cut down
to make the pews on which we sit. All the flowers of
the field amassed on the [   ] for which
I have no phrase. The wail walks me aisle to altar,
my English rigamortis stiff.

Tribute

I who never learned my grandmother's Creole, eulogize in French's
closest offering, forget the words instantly for what the French did to my
grandmother's kin. The pipe organ drowns out the wail's enrapture, a
jubilant juke by comparison, fades the Jobian O! My English, Lazarus,
rises again, dies again: English village born, Lower Saxony, 550 CE,
parents Anglo, Frisian survived by the ninety seconds I am a pallbearer,
part pillar, part stone face, one of six.

Coffin Dance

The white gloves idle softly on my hands. A dozen white roses usher
sarcophagus heaven-wise, up aisle to sunbeam. Another wail.
O, to die in summertime. To be buried in summertime. Hot city
corner, sedans honking down shimmering asphalt, band
of crickets, cicada brood. We, the burial party jostle, jazz
funeral, brass body, our English undead, stumbling, sickly
sweet, decomposing, recomposing as cemetery directions.
Behind the black gate we lower the [   ]
into the ground. Our English follows it into the ground,
a silent prayer. Our English, the flowers we throw in the grave:
Carnations, Chrysanthemums, Hydrangea, the white pallbearer
gloves. I drop one in the hole, slip the other in my pocket as a
memento—My grandfather sees this & sighs & shakes his head.

Kissing Song

cool of the cell phone pressed against my left cheek, kiss
       of the streetlight's glow
as a voice tells me I'm positive. This blow a kiss's opposite,
fading, the two-piece of the dial tone, jab, cross, combo into silence—

Silent, I recall every heat brush of mouth, red lipstick, loneliness.
In old pictures my parents collide, black plums prodigious before pit.
In 8th grade the Black boys already kiss the trick dice, lip lock with
      dead

presidents—I wonder which kiss cursed me? A peck with red plastic
      cups?
I recall two silhouettes at Navy Pier merging whole, began by
"k", texted casual, leading to *sing* in the alley—Trick question:

What land does this land become if I kiss lips that look like Emma
      Stone's
lips? Kiss of answers. A land that can kiss the blackest part of my ass.
How Black? My first kiss was in a church on the Southside of Chicago.

My first kiss tasted like Flamin' Hot Cheetos. I'd never heard "Kiss" by
Prince, yet my heart sang, *you don't have to be beautiful, while we this close.*
The other kids sang the song of me and Lisa sitting in a tree, our lips

a singular black fruit, the knowledge of good and evil. Trick answer:
Kiss was recorded in the April of the Chernobyl disaster
as radiation kissed thousands. Maybe all kisses spread some illness,

heavy metal, arsenic. When a white boy kissed my left cheek
at the house party, I bared Cheshire teeth as he fled
from my wild and became small—God, I was so fucking fragile

that whole week a mad masculine swearing I could kill, break any man
on the street. I think, *everyone's been betrayed by a person they've kissed.*
Perhaps evil persists attaching to sweetness—in parts of Sudan

it is believed the mouth is a portal to the soul.   They sidestep the
fevered impulse to avoid having their spirit snatched—It's likely part of
my soul lies with everyone I have kissed. Each pair of lips flashes

by like a float in a parade festooned with flowers, roses, violets,
the virus starts as a single point, increases to seven simplex
worth of connections. Where I got it from anyone's guess at this point.

There is no cure and yet, in front of me, in the dark, I see starlight
moonlight ebb through the window, two dark bodies
          enmeshed despite the dark.
Every time their glow reaches me, I'm infected with something endless.

Mother's Day at Crystal Banquet, Now Closed

I dance with my mother beneath the fake crystal
chandelier. A group of us swaying *kompa* in circles,
with our mothers, in honor of our mothers, despite
our mothers. We radiate out like the plastic floral
arrangements adorning each table, our endless
fractal orbit, Creole as sonic centerfold. I don't
understand what infects me, only know it does,
the iridescence of immortal flowers, the *kompa* band's
baritone, the blue as the *karabela* dresses river
down a makeshift runway. We have come to
pay respect to our mothers, our mother tongue
which heals, speaks for itself, is here in our collective
magnetic spin, our slew of aphorisms, our revolutionary
lilt, honed. All our mothers are here with us
our bodies & so their bodies raised mitochondrial.
& we have gathered to eat bread and chicken penne,
for *Tante Raymonde* to take my arm & lead me
to dance, for my cousin Michael to chase me,
this too a dance. He catches me, tickles my sides.
I am 8, sideways, a small infinity. My laughter is
in Creole. I laugh like no one is after me.

28 Years Later

the beef isn't dead—In '93 a mad cow roams,
auroch, auspicious. A mad Rome sends six ships
to enforce sanctions in Au Cap. To enforce democracy,
a road is unpaved in Al-Mansur. The cruise missile's
casualties "unknown," Schrodinger's civilians both alive,
buried—At this time, I both exist and don't. My mother's egg
having just met my father's seed, my body conceived
somewhere around the Ides of March. I'd like to think my soul's
conception occurred before, but it was definitely post-
Dew Breaker. I still remember its mitosis, how it brightened
witnessing Naomi build triumph on love: love. Watching
"Exterminate All the Brutes," how it reddened. 28 years later,
the beef undead, a set planning peace, a set planning hurt—

If there is an "us," it's those who made it out the quarantine
zone, those of us still in quarantine, those who didn't make it past 14.

All the Gifts

I.1

Enter anti-Eurydice, the room hot as underworld,
the room not a salon but what will do for now,
as you sit cross-legged on the floor, curls coiled
beneath the humid hood of July heat
& I think for once this play is not a tragedy,
this scene in which I don't speak but heed,
how to untwist each braid, my fingers learning
the language of hair: rat tail comb, protective style.
My left index, right index finger looping like lovers,
downward motion detangling each braid into darkling.

I.2

In this scene sunbeam, shadow, sunbeam. Enter ten fingers:

My Right Index Finger lit like:
>   *Girl! We gone have you looking*
>   *like Janet in poetic justice.*

My Left Index Finger [languid]
>   *I was there when they called you windowless room,*
>   *tomb. Our mamas said, if you don't have anything*

nice to say don't say nothing. So, you look like
beauty rest, like wildflowers awaiting sunrise.

My Left Middle Finger,
    [says nothing]

    In the background "m.a.a.d city," In the background:

My Right Middle Finger Most Honorable Phalanx raps:
    they killed our cousin back in '93
    they killed our cousin back in '94
    they killed our cousin back in '95
    they killed our cousin back in '96
    they killed our cousin back in '97
    they killed our cousin back in '98
    they killed our cousin back in '99
    they killed our cousin back in '00

My Left Ring Finger balances a rat tail comb scepter style,
stabs the X in a braid to unravel treasure, signs:
    It's not so much as fuck their peace
    as a truce is not peace.

My Right Thumb Sergeant of Arms,
[tugs a tuft behind the ear], reminds:
    your vengeance could be peace or a beautiful
    bewitching, poetic justice, a gorgon mane

petrifying fair features, a thousand Davids,
a museum of every mad city.

I.3
When I've finished the act,
our day is just beginning.

You say, *not bad*, ask me
how you look. I peep,

in spite of all the men
who feared turning to stone,

become something soft.

Acknowledgments

"The Tourist" *The Yale Review* (Sept. 2022)

"Mother's Day at Crystal Banquet, Now Closed" *Poetry Magazine* (Dec. 2021)

"American Monster" *Guernica Magazine* (Oct. 2021)

"The Brooms," "First Person Plural" *The Rumpus* (Oct. 2021)

"I feel most like a zombi after consuming a cocktail" *Kenyon Review* (July 2021)

"White Zombie" "Black Zombi" "The Deer" *Boulevard Magazine* (May 2021) Print.

"White Zombie" "Still Life: ˈblæknəs" *Apogee Journal* (Feb. 2021)

"Self-portrait of the artist as a Zombie" *Pleiades Magazine* (August 2020)

"Fever," "(un)dead," "Like," "Still Life: Roses in a Makeshift Vase" *The Adroit Journal* (March 2020)

Thank Yous

Thank you to the editors and journals where these poems previously appeared.

Thank you: To my family and friends. To my brother Jarett who we miss very much. To Uncle Ricky, Auntie Crystal, Auntie Jenny, and Auntie Shari. To my dad Harold. To my grandfather Edner and Granny Cubie. To my grandmother Denise, in loving memory. To Cherline. To my friends: Ola, Matthew, Annesha, Carlina, Austin, Eric, Eddie, Jasmine, and Kaila for both your friendship and your support of my work over the years.

To YCA and my undergraduate poetry professors Mark Jarman, Rick Hilles, and Melissa Pexa for showing me this could be a life. To the writers and readers whose insights helped shape these poems, especially Natalie and Shane McCrae. To my teachers and mentors in the HZWP especially A Van Jordan, Linda Gregerson, and Diane Seuss. To my cohort: Isabel, Kassy, Jennifer, Monica, Ian, Joumana, Sora, Mariya, and Michael. I'm eternally fortunate to have been in the same cohort as you. To my classmates with whom I've shared a workshop: Nadia, Ayo, David, Mary, Sara, Daniella, Augusta, Erika, Justin, Lorenzo; thank you for your keen eyes.

To my friends and colleagues at the Vermont Studio Center, especially Erin, Joan, Taneum, Rita, Rachel, and Connie. To my workshop at Tin House, especially: Zefyr, Donna, Kemi, Maria, and Samiya. To Conor and Scott from University College Dublin and Jonathan Moore. To my students, who I learn from all the time.

To the institutions that have supported the writing of these poems. To my friend and mentor Nate Marshall for believing in me. To my Brothers. To my mother, Kareen, for seeing me through.

Bryan Byrdlong is a Black poet from Chicago, Illinois. His debut poetry collection, *Strange Flowers,* was released from YesYes Books in 2025. He received his MFA in Creative Writing from the Helen Zell Writers Program and has been published in *Guernica Magazine, The Kenyon Review,* and *Poetry Magazine,* among others. Bryan received a 2021 Ruth Lilly and Dorothy Sargent Rosenberg Poetry Fellowship from the Poetry Foundation. He is currently a PhD student in Creative Writing at USC in Los Angeles.

Also from YesYes Books

FICTION

The Nothing by Lauren Davis

Girls Like Me by Nina Packebush

Three Queerdos and a Baby by Nina Packebush

WRITING RESOURCES

Gathering Voices: Creating a Community-Based Poetry Workshop
    by Marty McConnell

FULL-LENGTH COLLECTIONS

Ugly Music by Diannely Antigua

Bone Language by Jamaica Baldwin

Cataloguing Pain by Allison Blevins

What Runs Over by Kayleb Rae Candrilli

This, Sisyphus by Brandon Courtney

Salt Body Shimmer by Aricka Foreman

Gutter by Lauren Brazeal Garza

Forever War by Kate Gaskin

Inconsolable Objects by Nancy Miller Gomez

Ceremony of Sand by Rodney Gomez

Undoll by Tanya Grae

Loudest When Startled by luna rey hall

Everything Breaking / For Good by Matt Hart

40 WEEKS by Julia Kolchinsky

Sons of Achilles by Nabila Lovelace

Otherlight by Jill Mceldowney

Landscape with Sex and Violence by Lynn Melnick

Refusenik by Lynn Melnick

GOOD MORNING AMERICA I AM HUNGRY AND ON FIRE
by jamie mortara

Stay by Tanya Olson

Born Backwards by Tanya Olson

a falling knife has no handle by Emily O'Neill

To Love An Island by Ana Portnoy Brimmer

Another Way to Split Water by Alycia Pirmohamed

Tell This to the Universe by Katie Prince

One God at a Time by Meghan Privitello

I'm So Fine: A List of Famous Men & What I Had On by Khadijah Queen

If the Future Is a Fetish by Sarah Sgro

Gilt by Raena Shirali

Say It Hurts by Lisa Summe

Boat Burned by Kelly Grace Thomas

Helen Or My Hunger by Gale Marie Thompson

As She Appears by Shelley Wong

RECENT CHAPBOOK COLLECTIONS

Vinyl 45s

Exit Pastoral by Aidan Forster

Crown for the Girl Inside by Lisa Low

Of Darkness and Tumbling by Mónica Gomery

Phantasmagossip by Sara Mae

Juned by Jenn Marie Nunes

Year of the Sheep by Stacey Park

Scavenger by Jessica Lynn Suchon

Unmonstrous by John Allen Taylor

Preparing the Body by Norma Liliana Valdez

Giantess by Emily Vizzo

Blue Note Editions

Kissing Caskets by Mahogany L. Browne

One Above One Below: Positions & Lamentations by Gala Mukomolova

The Porch (As Sanctuary) by Jae Nichelle